FIRST 50 MELODIES
YOU SHOULD PLAY ON GUITAR

ISBN 978-1-7051-9311-2

HAL•LEONARD®

Visit Hal Leonard Online at
www.halleonard.com

World headquarters, contact:
Hal Leonard
7777 West Bluemound Road
Milwaukee, WI 53213
Email: info@halleonard.com

In Europe, contact:
Hal Leonard Europe Limited
1 Red Place
London, W1K 6PL
Email: info@halleonardeurope.com

In Australia, contact:
Hal Leonard Australia Pty. Ltd.
4 Lentara Court
Cheltenham, Victoria, 3192 Australia
Email: info@halleonard.com.au

The A Team

Words and Music by Ed Sheeran

Chorus

just un-der the up-per hand and go mad for a cou-ple grams.

And she don't want to go _____ out - side to - night. ___ And in a

pipe she flies to the moth-er-land or sells love to an - oth-er man.

To Coda 1 ⊕
To Coda 2 ⊕

It's too cold _____ out - side _____ for an - gels ___ to fly. ___

Interlude

___ An - gels ___ to fly. ___

D.C. al Coda 1

⊕ **Coda 1**

Bridge

___ An an - gel ___ will die, ___ cov-ered in ___ white.

Closed eye ___ and hop-ing for a bet - ter life. _____ This ___

3

Additional Lyrics

2. Ripped gloves, raincoat.
Tried to swim to stay 'float.
Dry house, wet clothes.
Loose change, bank notes.
Weary-eyed, dry throat.
Call girl, no phone.

Addams Family Theme

Theme from the TV Show and Movie
Music and Lyrics by Vic Mizzy

ABC

Words and Music by Alphonso Mizell, Frederick Perren, Deke Richards and Berry Gordy

Amazing Grace

Words by John Newton
Traditional American Melody

Additional Lyrics

2. 'Twas grace that taught my heart to fear,
   And grace my fears relieved.
   How precious did that grace appear
   The hour I first believed.

3. Through many dangers, toils and snares,
   I have already come.
   'Tis grace has brought me safe thus far,
   And grace will lead me home.

4. The Lord has promised good to me,
   His word my hope secures.
   He will my shield and portion be
   As long as life endures.

5. And when this flesh and heart shall fail,
   And mortal life shall cease,
   I shall posess within the veil
   A life of joy and peace.

6. When we've been there ten thousand years,
   Bright shining as the sun.
   We've no less days to sing God's praise
   Than when we first begun.

Axel F

Theme from the Paramount Motion Picture BEVERLY HILLS COP
By Harold Faltermeyer

And I Love Her

Words and Music by John Lennon and Paul McCartney

⊕ Coda

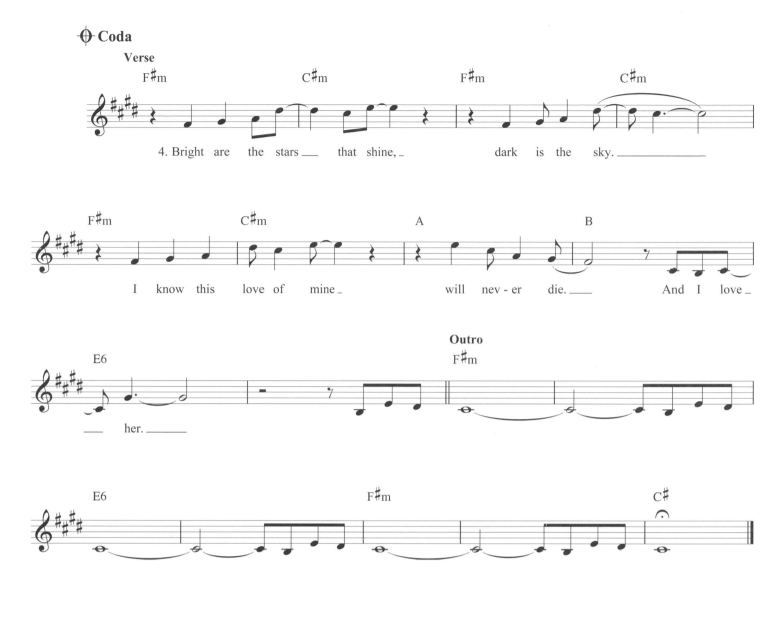

Additional Lyrics

2. She gives me ev'rything, and tenderly.
   This kiss my lover brings she brings to me.
   And I love her.

3. Bright are the stars that shine, dark is the sky.
   I know this love of mine will never die.
   And I love her.

Baby Shark

Traditional Nursery Rhyme
Arranged by Pinkfong and KidzCastle

Verse

Moderately

1. Ba - by shark, do, do, do, do, ___ do, do. Ba - by shark, do, do, do, do, ___ do, do. Ba - by
3., 5. *See additional lyrics*

shark, do, do, do, do, ___ do, do. Ba - by shark. 2. Mom - my
4., 6. *See additional lyrics*

Verse

shark, do, do, do, do, ___ do, do. Mom - my shark, do, do, do, do, ___ do, do. Mom - my

1., 2.

shark, do, do, do, do, ___ do, do. Mom - my shark. 3. Dad - dy

3.

Verse

hunt. 7. Run a - way, do, do, do, do, ___ do, do. Run a -
8. *See additional lyrics*

way, do, do, do, do, ___ do, do. Run a - way, do, do, do, do, ___ do, do. Run a -

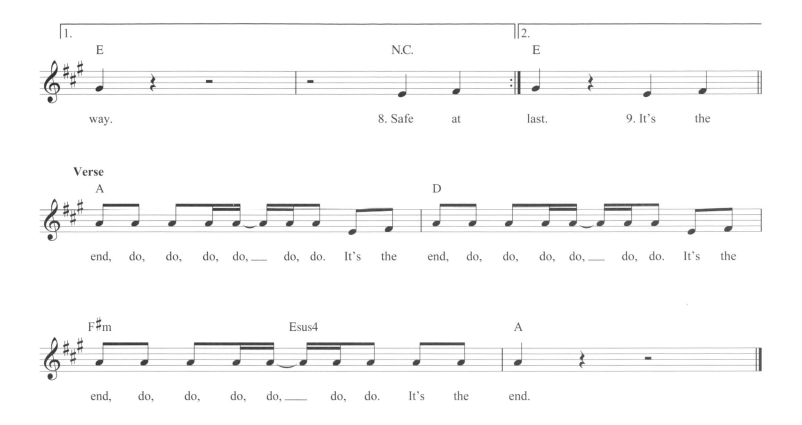

Additional Lyrics

3. Daddy shark, do, do, do, do, do, do.
   Daddy shark, do, do, do, do, do, do.
   Daddy shark, do, do, do, do, do, do.
   Daddy shark.

4. Grandma shark, do, do, do, do, do, do.
   Grandma shark, do, do, do, do, do, do.
   Grandma shark, do, do, do, do, do, do.
   Grandma shark.

5. Grandpa shark, do, do, do, do, do, do.
   Grandpa shark, do, do, do, do, do, do.
   Grandpa shark, do, do, do, do, do, do.
   Grandpa shark.

6. Let's go hunt, do, do, do, do, do, do.
   Let's go hunt, do, do, do, do, do, do.
   Let's go hunt, do, do, do, do, do, do.
   Let's go hunt.

8. Safe at last, do, do, do, do, do, do.
   Safe at last, do, do, do, do, do, do.
   Safe at last, do, do, do, do, do, do.
   Safe at last.

Blinding Lights

Words and Music by Abel Tesfaye, Max Martin, Jason Quenneville, Oscar Holter and Ahmad Balshe

Additional Lyrics

3. I'm running out of time,
   'Cause I can see the sun light up the sky.
   So I hit the road in overdrive, baby.

Can't Help Falling in Love

from the Paramount Picture BLUE HAWAII

Words and Music by George David Weiss, Hugo Peretti and Luigi Creatore

Additional Lyrics

2. Shall I stay?
   Would it be a sin
   If I can't help falling in love with you?

Canon in D

By Johann Pachelbel

Slowly

Circles

Words and Music by Austin Post, Kaan Gunesberk, Louis Bell, William Walsh and Adam Feeney

Do-Re-Mi

from THE SOUND OF MUSIC
Lyrics by Oscar Hammerstein II
Music by Richard Rodgers

Don't Stop Believin'

Words and Music by Steve Perry, Neal Schon and Jonathan Cain

Additional Lyrics

2. Just a city boy, born and raised in south Detroit.
   He took the midnight train goin' anywhere.

Chorus 2., 4. Streetlights, people; living just to find emotion.
   Hiding somewhere in the night.

5. Some will win, some will lose. Some are born to sing the blues.
   Oh, the movie never ends. It goes on and on and on and on.

Eine Kleine Nachtmusik, K. 525

By Wolfgang Amadeus Mozart

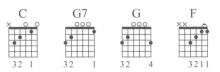

Moderately fast

Fly Me to the Moon
(In Other Words)

Words and Music by Bart Howard

Additional Lyrics

2. Fill my heart with song
And let me sing forevermore.
You are all I long for,
All I worship and adore.
In other words, please be true.
In other words, I love you.

Für Elise, WoO 59

By Ludwig van Beethoven

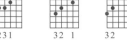

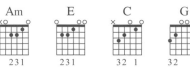

Slowly

Happy Birthday to You

Words and Music by Mildred J. Hill and Patty S. Hill

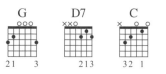

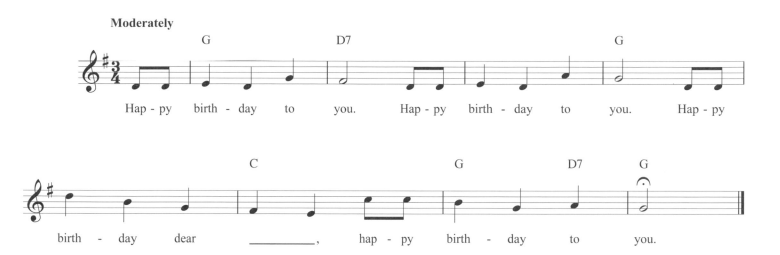

Hap-py birth-day to you. Hap-py birth-day to you. Hap-py

birth-day dear _____, hap-py birth-day to you.

Good Vibrations

Words and Music by Brian Wilson and Mike Love

A

I'm pick-in' up good vi - bra - tions. She's giv - in' me the ex - ci - ta - tions.

B

I'm pick-in' up good vi - bra - tions. She's giv - in' me the ex - ci - ta - tions.

Interlude
Slower

G   Am   D

Bridge

G   Am   D

Got - ta keep ___ those lov - in' good vi - bra - tions a hap-pen - in' with her. ___

2nd time, D.S. and fade

G   Am   D

Got - ta keep ___ those lov - in' good vi - bra - tions a hap-pen - in' with her. ___

Additional Lyrics

2. Close my eyes; she's somehow closer now.
   Softly smile, I know she must be kind.
   When I look in her eyes,
   She goes with me to a blossom room.

Hallelujah

Words and Music by Leonard Cohen

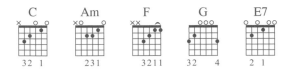

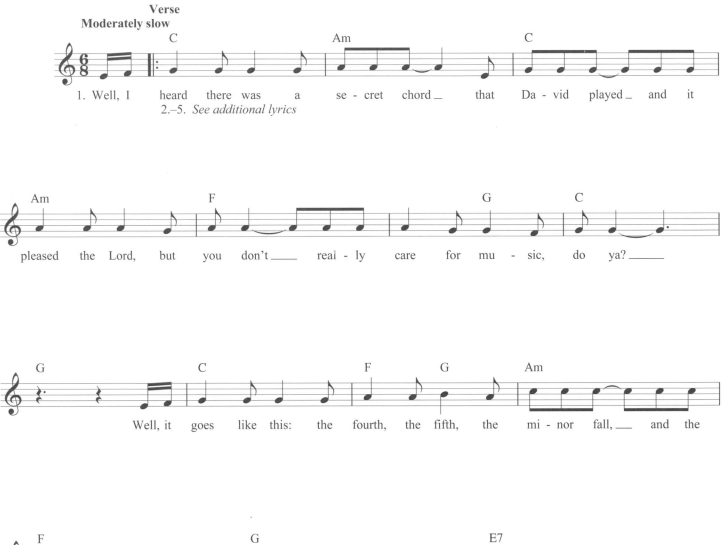

Verse
Moderately slow

1. Well, I heard there was a se-cret chord __ that Da-vid played __ and it
2.–5. *See additional lyrics*

pleased the Lord, but you don't ___ real-ly care for mu-sic, do ya? ___

Well, it goes like this: the fourth, the fifth, the mi-nor fall, __ and the

ma-jor lift, the baf-fled king ___ com-pos-ing ___ Hal-le-

Chorus

lu - jah. ___ Hal-le-lu-jah, ___ hal-le-

Am

lu - jah, _____ hal - le - lu - jah, _____ hal - le -

1. - 4.
C   G   C   Am

lu   -   jah.

C   Am   ‖ 5.
                                                    C   G

2. Well, your   lu   -   jah.   Hal - le -

Outro-Chorus
F   Am   F

lu - jah. _____   Hal - le - lu - jah. _____   Hal - le - lu - jah. _____

                    C   G   C

_____   Hal - le - lu   -   jah. _____

Additional Lyrics

2. Well, your faith was strong, but you needed proof.
You saw her bathing on the roof.
Her beauty and the moonlight overthrew ya.
She tied you to her kitchen chair,
And she broke your throne and she cut your hair,
And from your lips she drew the hallelujah.

3. Well, baby, I've been here before,
I've seen this room and I've walked this floor.
You know, I used to live alone before I knew ya.
And I've seen your flag on the marble arch,
And love is not a vict'ry march,
It's a cold and it's a broken hallelujah.

4. Well, there was a time when you let me know
What's really going on below.
But now you never show that to me, do ya?
But remember when I moved in you
And the holy dove was moving too,
And ev'ry breath we drew was hallelujah.

5. Maybe there is a God above,
But all I've ever learned from love
Was how to shoot somebody who outdrew ya.
And it's not a cry that you hear at night,
It's not somebody who's seen the light,
It's a cold and it's a broken hallelujah.

Havana

Words and Music by Camila Cabello, Louis Bell, Pharrell Williams, Adam Feeney, Ali Tamposi,
Jeffery Lamar Williams, Brian Lee, Andrew Wotman, Brittany Hazzard and Kaan Gunesberk

Heart and Soul

from the Paramount Short Subject A SONG IS BORN

Words by Frank Loesser
Music by Hoagy Carmichael

Additional Lyrics

2., 5. Heart and soul, I begged to be adored.
Lost control and tumbled overboard;
Gladly. That magic night we kissed
There in the moonmist.

Hotel California

Words and Music by Don Henley, Glenn Frey and Don Felder

Additional Lyrics

2. There she stood in the doorway; I heard the mission bell.
   And I was thinkin' to myself this could be heaven or this could be hell.
   Then she lit up her candle and she showed me the way.
   There were voices down the corridor, I thought I heard them say:

3. Her mind is Tiffany-twisted. She got the Mercedes Benz. Uh.
   She got a lot of pretty, pretty boys that she calls friends.
   How they dance in the courtyard, sweet summer sweat.
   Some dance to remember; some dance to forget.

4. So I called up the captain, "Please bring me my wine."
   He said, "We haven't had that spirit here since nineteen-sixty-nine."
   And still those voices are calling from far away.
   Wake you up in the middle of the night just to hear them say, ay:

5. Mirrors on the ceiling, the pink champagne on ice.
   And she said, "We are all just prisoners here of our own device."
   And in the master's chambers they gathered for the feast.
   They stab it with their steely knives, but they just can't kill the beast.

6. Last thing I remember I was running for the door.
   I had to find the passage back to the place I was before.
   "Relax," said the nightman, "We are programmed to receive.
   You can check out anytime you like but you can never leave."

I Want It That Way

Words and Music by Max Martin and Andreas Carlsson

Imagine

Words and Music by John Lennon

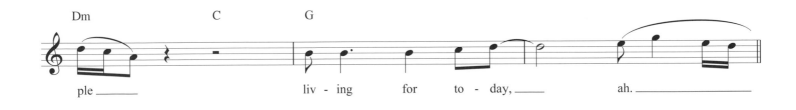

2. I-mag-ine there's no coun-tries, it is-n't hard to do;

3. *See additional lyrics*

Additional Lyrics

3. Imagine no possessions;
   I wonder if you can.
   No need for greed or hunger,
   A brotherhood of man.
   Imagine all the people sharing all the world.

The Imperial March
(Darth Vader's Theme)

from STAR WARS: THE EMPIRE STRIKES BACK
Music by John Williams

Moderately

Jeopardy Theme

Music by Merv Griffin

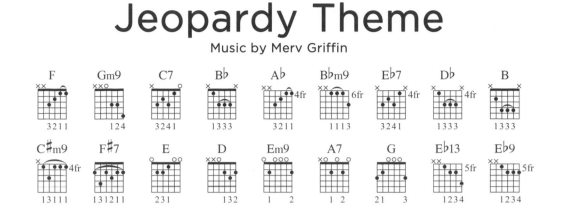

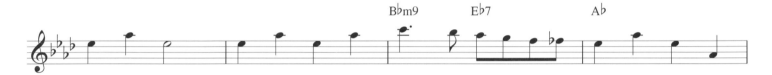

43

Theme from "Jurassic Park"

from the Universal Motion Picture JURASSIC PARK
Composed by John Williams

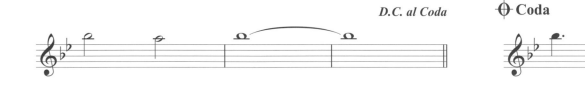

Minuet in G

from THE ANNA MAGDALENA NOTEBOOK (originally for keyboard)
By Johann Sebastian Bach

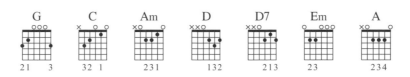

45

Lean on Me

Words and Music by Bill Withers

Verse
Slowly

1. Some - times in our lives, ___ we all have pain, ___ we all have sor - rows. ___ But if we are wise, ___ we know that there's ___ ___ al - ways to - mor - row. ___ Lean on me ___ when you're not strong. ___ And I'll be your friend, ___ I'll help you car - ry on, ___ For it won't be long ___ till I'm gon - na need ___ some - bod - y to lean ___

Let It Be

Words and Music by John Lennon and Paul McCartney

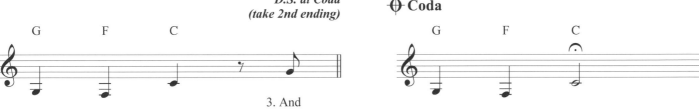

Additional Lyrics

2. And when the broken-hearted people living in the world agree,
There will be an answer, let it be.
For, though they may be parted, there is still a chance that they will see
There will be an answer, let it be.

3. And when the night is cloudy, there is still a light that shines on me.
Shine until tomorrow, let it be.
I wake up to the sound of music, Mother Mary comes to me
Speaking words of wisdom, let it be.

Linus and Lucy

from A CHARLIE BROWN CHRISTMAS

By Vince Guaraldi

D

E

Mission: Impossible Theme

from the Paramount Television Series MISSION: IMPOSSIBLE

By Lalo Schifrin

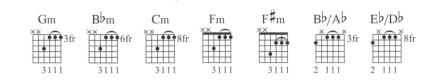

Over the Rainbow

from THE WIZARD OF OZ
Music by Harold Arlen
Lyric by E.Y. "Yip" Harburg

Additional Lyrics

2. Somewhere over the rainbow, skies are blue.
   And the dreams that you dare to dream really do come true.

3. Somewhere over the rainbow, bluebirds fly.
   Birds fly over the rainbow; why, then, oh why, can't I?

My Heart Will Go On
(Love Theme from 'Titanic')

from the Paramount and Twentieth Century Fox Motion Picture TITANIC

Music by James Horner
Lyric by Will Jennings

Additional Lyrics

2. Love can touch us one time and last for a lifetime.
   And never let go till we're gone.
   Love was when I loved you; one true time I hold to.
   In my life we'll always go on.

Perfect

Words and Music by Ed Sheeran

Additional Lyrics

2. Well, I found a woman, stronger than anyone I know.
   She shares my dreams, I hope that someday, I'll share her home.
   I found a love to carry more than just my secrets,
   To carry love, to carry children of our own.

Pre-Chorus We are still kids, but we're so in love, fighting against all odds.
   I know we'll be all right this time.
   Darling, just hold my hand; be my girl, I'll be your man.
   I've seen the future in your eyes.

Chorus Baby, I'm dancing in the dark with you between my arms.
   Barefoot on the grass, listening to our fav'rite song.
   When I saw you in that dress looking so beautiful,
   I don't deserve this. Darling, you look perfect tonight.

The Pink Panther

from THE PINK PANTHER
By Henry Mancini

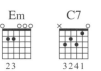

Shallow

from A STAR IS BORN

Words and Music by Stefani Germanotta, Mark Ronson, Andrew Wyatt and Anthony Rossomando

Outro-Chorus

Additional Lyrics

2. Tell me something, boy:
   Aren't you tired, tryin' to fill that void,
   Or do you need more?
   Ain't it hard keeping it so hardcore?

A Sky Full of Stars

Words and Music by Guy Berryman, Jon Buckland, Will Champion, Chris Martin and Tim Bergling

I think I { saw / see } you. _____

1. 2.

I think I see you. _____

Interlude

Outro

'Cause you're a sky, _____

_____ you're a sky _____ full of stars, ____ such a heav-en-ly view. _____

You're such a heav-en-ly view. _____

Play 3 times

Additional Lyrics

2. 'Cause you're a sky, 'cause you're a sky full of stars.
   I wanna die in your arms.
   'Cause you get lighter the more it gets dark.
   I'm gonna give you my heart.

63

The Sound of Silence

Words and Music by Paul Simon

si - lent rain-drops fell, and ech - oed in the

wells of si - lence. 5. And the peo - ple bowed and

Verse

prayed to the ne - on god they made.

And the sign flashed out its _____ warn - ing _____ in the words that it was _

_ form - ing, _ and the signs said, "The words of the pro - phets are

writ - ten on the sub - way walls and ten - e - ment halls" and

whis-per'd in the sounds of si - lence.

Additional Lyrics

3. And in the naked light I saw
   Ten thousand people; maybe more.
   People talking without speaking,
   People hearing without list'ning.
   People writing songs
   That voices never share,
   And no one dare
   Disturb the sound of silence.

SpongeBob SquarePants Theme Song

from SPONGEBOB SQUAREPANTS

Words and Music by Mark Harrison, Blaise Smith, Stephen M. Hillenburg and Derek Drymon

Sweet Caroline

Words and Music by Neil Diamond

Additional Lyrics

2. Look at the night, and it don't seem so lonely;
   We fill it up with only two.
   And when I hurt, hurtin' runs off my shoulder.
   How can I hurt when holding you?

Pre-Chorus Warm, touchin' warm,
   Reachin' out;
   Touchin' me, touchin' you.

A Thousand Years

from the Summit Entertainment film THE TWILIGHT SAGA: BREAKING DAWN - PART 1
Words and Music by David Hodges and Christina Perri

Additional Lyrics

2. Time stands still. Beauty in all she is.
I will be brave. I will not let anything
Take away what's standing in front of me.
Every breath, every hour has come to this.

Tomorrow

from the Musical Production ANNIE

Lyric by Martin Charnin
Music by Charles Strouse

Outro-Verse

Additional Lyrics

2. Just thinking about tomorrow
   Clears away the cobwebs and the sorrow.
   Till there's none.

Unchained Melody

from the Motion Picture UNCHAINED
Lyric by Hy Zaret
Music by Alex North

VeggieTales Theme Song

Words and Music by Mike Nawrocki and Lisa Vischer

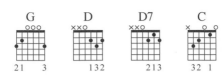

Moderately

If you like to

talk to to - ma - toes, if a squash can make you smile,

if you like to waltz with po - ta - toes up and down the

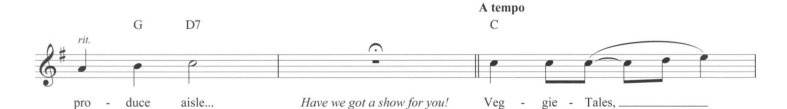

pro - duce aisle... *Have we got a show for you!* Veg - gie - Tales, _____

Veg - gie - Tales, _____ Veg - gie - Tales, _____ Veg - gie - Tales. _____

Veg - gie - Tales, _____ Veg - gie - Tales, _____ Veg - gie - Tales, _____

What a Wonderful World

Words and Music by George David Weiss and Bob Thiele

Wonderful Tonight

Words and Music by Eric Clapton

Additional Lyrics

2. We go to a party, and ev'ryone turns to see
   This beautiful lady that's walking around with me.
   And then she asks me, "Do you feel alright?"
   And I say, "Yes, I feel wonderful tonight."

3. It's time to go home now, and I've got an aching head.
   So I give her the car keys and she helps me to bed.
   And then I tell her, as I turn out the light,
   I say, "My darling, you were wonderful tonight."

You Are My Sunshine

Words and Music by Jimmie Davis

Additional Lyrics

2. I'll always love you and make you happy
   If you will only say the same.
   But if you leave me to love another,
   You'll regret it all some day.

3. You told me once, dear, you really loved me
   And no one else could come between.
   But now you've left me and love another;
   You have shattered all my dreams.

You Raise Me Up

Words and Music by Brendan Graham and Rolf Løvland

2. You raise me

Verse

up so I can stand on moun - tains. You raise me up to walk on storm - y

seas. I am strong when I am on ___ your shoul - ders. You raise me

up to more than I ___ can ___ be. You raise me

Outro-Verse

up so I can stand ___ on moun - tains. You raise me up to walk on storm - y

1.

seas. I ___ am ___ strong ___ when I am on ___ your shoul - ders. You raise me

2.

up to more than I ___ can be. You raise me seas. I am

strong ___ when I am on ___ your ___ shoul - ders. ___ You raise me

up to more than I ___ can ___ be. You raise me

up to more than I ___ can ___ be. ___

85

Star Wars
(Main Theme)

from STAR WARS: A NEW HOPE
Music by John Williams

RHYTHM TAB LEGEND

Rhythm Tab is a form of notation that adds rhythmic values to the traditional tab staff.

TABLATURE graphically represents the guitar fingerboard. Each horizontal line represents a string, and each number represents a fret. Rhythmic values are shown using ovals, stems, and dots.

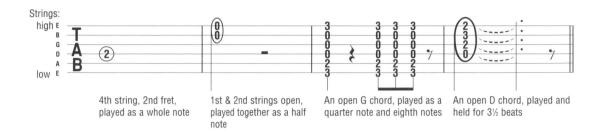

4th string, 2nd fret, played as a whole note

1st & 2nd strings open, played together as a half note

An open G chord, played as a quarter note and eighth notes

An open D chord, played and held for 3½ beats

Definitions for Special Guitar Notation

HALF-STEP BEND: Strike the note and bend up 1/2 step.

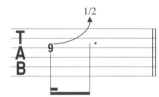

WHOLE-STEP BEND: Strike the note and bend up one step.

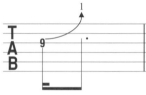

SLIGHT (MICROTONE) BEND: Strike the note and bend up 1/4 step.

BEND AND RELEASE: Strike the note and bend up as indicated, then release back to the original note. Only the first note is struck.

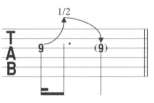

PRE-BEND: Bend the note as indicated, then strike it.

GRACE NOTE PRE-BEND AND RELEASE: Bend the note as indicated. Strike it and release the bend back to the original note.

UNISON BEND: Strike the two notes simultaneously and bend the lower note up to the pitch of the higher.

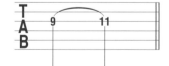

HOLD BEND: While sustaining bent note, strike note on different string.

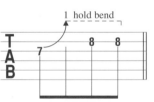

VIBRATO: The string is vibrated by rapidly bending and releasing the note with the fretting hand.

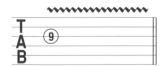

WIDE VIBRATO: The pitch is varied to a greater degree by vibrating with the fretting hand.

HAMMER-ON: Strike the first (lower) note with one finger, then sound the higher note (on the same string) with another finger by fretting it without picking.

PULL-OFF: Place both fingers on the notes to be sounded. Strike the first note and without picking, pull the finger off to sound the second (lower) note.

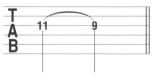

HAMMER FROM NOWHERE: Sound note(s) by hammering with fret hand finger only.

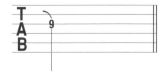

GRACE NOTE SLUR: Strike the note and immediately hammer-on (or pull-off) as indicated.

GRACE NOTE SLUR (CLUSTER): Strike the notes and immediately hammer-on (or pull-off) as indicated.

LEGATO SLIDE: Strike the first note and then slide the same fret-hand finger up or down to the second note. The second note is not struck.

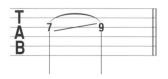

SHIFT SLIDE: Same as legato slide, except the second note is struck.

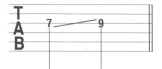

GRACE NOTE SLIDE: Quickly slide into the note from below or above.

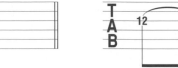

TRILL: Very rapidly alternate between the notes indicated by continuously hammering on and pulling off.

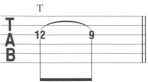

TAPPING: Hammer ("tap") the fret indicated with the pick-hand index or middle finger and pull off to the note fretted by the fret hand.

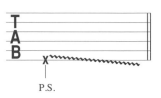

NATURAL HARMONIC: Strike the note while the fret-hand lightly touches the string directly over the fret indicated.

Harm.

PINCH HARMONIC: The note is fretted normally and a harmonic is produced by adding the edge of the thumb or the tip of the index finger of the pick hand to the normal pick attack.

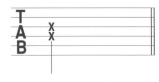

P.H.

HARP HARMONIC: The note is fretted normally and a harmonic is produced by gently resting the pick hand's index finger directly above the indicated fret (in parentheses) while the pick hand's thumb or pick assists by plucking the appropriate string.

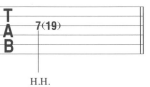

H.H.

PICK SCRAPE: The edge of the pick is rubbed down (or up) the string, producing a scratchy sound.

P.S.

MUFFLED STRINGS: A percussive sound is produced by laying the fret hand across the string(s) without depressing, and striking them with the pick hand.

PALM MUTING: The note is partially muted by the pick hand lightly touching the string(s) just before the bridge.

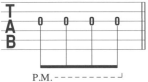

P.M. - - - - - - - - - ⌐

RAKE: Drag the pick across the strings indicated with a single motion.

rake - ⌐

TREMOLO PICKING: The note is picked as rapidly and continuously as possible.

ARPEGGIATE: Play the notes of the chord indicated by quickly rolling them from bottom to top.

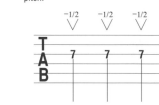

VIBRATO BAR DIVE AND RETURN: The pitch of the note or chord is dropped a specified number of steps (in rhythm), then returned to the original pitch.

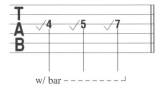

w/ bar

VIBRATO BAR SCOOP: Depress the bar just before striking the note, then quickly release the bar.

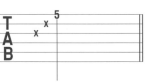

w/ bar - - - - - - - ⌐

VIBRATO BAR DIP: Strike the note and then immediately drop a specified number of steps, then release back to the original pitch.

w/ bar - - - - - - - ⌐

Additional Musical Definitions

(accent) • Accentuate note (play it louder)

(staccato) • Play the note short

(fermata) • A hold or pause

⊓ • Downstroke

∨ • Upstroke

• Repeat measures between signs

NOTE: Tablature numbers in parentheses are used when:
- The note is sustained, but a new articulation begins (such as a hammer-on, pull-off, slide, or bend), or
- A bend is released.
- A note sustains while crossing from one staff to another.